LOW CALORIE COOKING

LOW CALORIE COOKING

Rano Suri

wisdom tree

First published 2008
Reprinted November 2008

Photographs: Ashish Chawla
Cover: Tikka Acharia

ISBN 81-8328-081-1

Published by
Wisdom Tree
4779/23 Ansari Road
Darya Ganj, New Delhi-110002
Ph.: 23247966/67/68

Published by Shobit Arya for Wisdom Tree; *edited by* Manju Gupta; *designed by* Kamal P. Jammual; *typeset at* Marks & Strokes, New Delhi-110002 and *printed at* Print Perfect, New Delhi-110064

CONTENTS

HOT-SHOT BREAKFAST

Ingredients

1 small carrot chopped into bits
½ cup finely chopped beans
½ cup peas
1 cup shredded cabbage
1 onion, finely chopped
½ tsp red chilli powder
½ tsp turmeric powder
½ tsp *kasuri methi*
½ tsp roasted ground *jeera* (cumin seeds)
1 tsp salt
½ tsp sugar
½ tsp *kalonji* (onion seeds)
3 tsp (1 tbsp) oil
½ tsp mustard seeds
250 gms *chirwa* (beaten rice)
4 tsp lemon juice

Contd.

• *Servings 6 persons* • *Preparation time 15 mins.* • *Cooking time 15 mins.*

Per Serving • *Protein (gms) 8.3* • *Fat (gms) 5* • *Fibre (gms) 2.4* • *Calories 210*

- Blanch carrot, beans and peas together in salted water. Pass this through a sieve.
- Heat oil, add mustard seeds, *jeera* and *kalonji*. Cook till the mustard seeds crackle.
- Add onion and cook for two minutes.
- Add red chilli powder, turmeric powder and *kasuri methi*. Stir it.
- Wash *chirwa* in a strainer and keep aside for one minute.
- Add carrot, beans, peas and cabbage.
- Cook for one minute. Add washed *chirwa*, salt, coriander leaves and sugar.
- Mix thoroughly. Cook till properly mixed. Add lemon juice.

Contd.

4 tsp coriander leaves
6 warm vegetable wraps or thin 8" *chappatis*

- Divide the mixture into six portions. Now place each portion in each warm *chappati*. Wrap and fold it.
- Serve hot. It is a healthy and low-fat breakfast or brunch.

LOW-CALORIE VEGETABLE WRAPS

Ingredients
2 cups *aata* (wheat flour)
1 cup *suji* (semolina)
½ tsp salt
1 tsp olive oil
Lukewarm water as required

Filling
1 spring onion chopped finely
100 gms blanched beans
1 big carrot chopped into bits
100 gms mushroom, finely chopped
1 cup cooked corns
1 tomato chopped into bits
1 tsp olive oil
1 tsp crushed garlic

Contd.

• *Servings 6 persons* • *Preparation time 30 mins.* • *Cooking time 15 mins.*
Per Serving • *Protein (gms) 8* • *Fat (gms) 4* • *Fibre (gms) 4* • *Calories 150*

- Sieve *aata*, *suji* and salt together. Add olive oil; mix well. Gradually add lukewarm water. Make a smooth and soft dough. Keep it covered for 30 minutes.
- Again knead it for three to four minutes to make it more soft.

FILLING

- Grease the pan with olive oil. Add garlic and stir it. Add onion. Cook for half a minute. Add beans, carrots, corn, green chillies, mushrooms and tomato. Cook for a minute.
- Then add tomato paste, salt, sugar and oregano. Mix well, cover and cook on slow fire for four minutes.
- Remove the lid and again cook for a minute.

Contd.

2 green chopped chillies
2 tsp chopped coriander leaves
4 tsp tomato paste
1 tsp salt
½ tsp sugar
A pinch of oregano (optional)

- Remove from fire. Sprinkle coriander leaves on top.
- Make medium-size balls from the dough. Roll into thin 6" *chappatis*.
- Heat a non-stick *tava* (griddle). Pour ½ tsp oil and wipe the *tava* with onion slice to make it smooth. Now lightly cook *chappati* on a medium flame. Wrap them with a dry napkin.
- Fill the *chappati* wrap with the prepared filling and fold it. Serve hot with sour hung-curd dip or salsa.

Ingredients
350 gms *paneer* made from skimmed milk
1 capsicum, diced into 1" pieces
1 onion, diced into 1" pieces
1 tomato (only skin) diced into 1" pieces
2 medium size boiled potatoes, sliced into 1" cubes

Marinade
1 tsp salt (level)
½ tsp red chilli powder
1 tsp coriander powder
1 tsp *kasuri methi*
½ tsp *amchur* (mango powder)

Contd.

TIKKA ACHARIA

• *Servings 6 persons* • *Preparation time 20 mins. + marination time* • *Roasting time 12 mins.*

Per Serving • *Protein (gms) 11* • *Fat (gms) 4* • *Fibre (gms) 4* • *Calories 150*

- Cut *paneer* into 1" cubes.
- In a large bowl, put together *paneer*, capsicum, onion, potatoes and tomatoes.
- Marinate them with all the ingredients given under marinade for half an hour.
- Grease the skewers (iron rods) and arrange one *paneer* cube, then onion, tomato and again a *paneer* cube.
- Add capsicum, onion, potato cube, tomato and capsicum pieces. Last of all, fix a *paneer* cube.
- Similarly arrange other skewers.
- Arrange them in a pre-heated oven at 220°C to roast for 12 minutes (or bake) till golden brown.

Contd.

1 tsp *saunf* (ground aniseed)
3 tsp lemon juice
2 tsp oil
½ tsp sugar

Tempering
2 tsp oil
½ tsp mustard seeds
½ tsp *kalonji* (onion seeds)
A pinch of *garam masala*
Roasted ground *jeera*

- Arrange them on a bed of cooked rice or lettuce leaves.
- Sprinkle roasted ground *jeera*.
- Heat oil, add mustard seeds, *kalonji*. Cook till the mustard seeds crackle.
- Add *garam masala*. Stir and immediately pour on *tikka acharia*.
- Sprinkle lemon juice and immediately serve.

STUFFED CAPSICUM

Ingredients

4 medium size capsicums (bellpepper) or 1 red, 2 green and 1 yellow capsicums
1 cup boiled and drained rice
½ cup boiled peas
1 small finely chopped onion
2 tsp olive oil
2 crushed garlic cloves
½ tsp black pepper
1 tsp salt
½ cup grated *paneer* made from skimmed milk
1 small finely chopped tomato
½ cup crushed cornflakes
Coriander leaves

• Servings 6 persons • Preparation time 15 mins. • Cooking time 5 mins. + Baking time 10 mins.

Per Serving • Protein (gms) 6 • Fat (gms) 5 • Fibre (gms) 2.1 • Calories 150

- Cut the capsicum horizontally. Rub 1 tsp olive oil on the outer side. Keep these under the grill till the capsicum skin is charred.
- Grease a pan with 1 tsp oil. Add garlic and onion. Cook for one minute.
- Add chopped tomato. Cook for half a minute.
- Mix boiled rice, peas, grated cottage cheese, salt and black pepper in it. Cook for a minute and remove from fire. Cool the mixture.
- Stuff the capsicums with the prepared mixture.
- Sprinkle crushed cornflakes on them. Bake in a pre-heated oven at 200°C for seven minutes till nicely golden brown. Garnish with coriander leaves.
- Serve hot with crisp toasted wheat bread.

DRY PEAS & CHANNA DAL

Ingredients
1 cup *channa dal* (black gram lentil)
1½ cup peas
1 tbsp oil (3 tsp)
½ tsp *jeera* (cumin seeds)
1 finely chopped onion
½ tsp red chilli powder
½ tsp *haldi* (turmeric powder)
1 tsp salt
1 tsp coriander powder

Contd.

• *Servings 6 persons* • *Preparation time 25 mins. + soaking time* • *Cooking time 20 mins.*
Per Serving *Protein (gms) 20* • *Fat (gms) 3* • *Fibre (gms) 6* • *Calories 180*

- Soak *channa dal* for four hours.
- Boil water along with salt. Add peas, cover the lid and remove from fire. Keep for five minutes.
- Pass this through a sieve and keep the water aside.
- Heat oil in a pressure cooker. Add *jeera*.
- Cook till the *jeera* crackles. Add onion and cook for four minutes.
- Add red chilli powder, coriander powder, turmeric powder and *garam masala*.
- Mix and add washed and soaked *dal* (drained) and add peas.

Contd.

Low-calorie Vegetable Wraps ➤

Overleaf Tikka Acharia

½ tsp *garam masala*
2 green chillies
Chopped coriander leaves
Lemon juice

- Sauté this for four minutes. Add 2½ cups of reserved water. Cook till it boils.
- Add salt and again cook for a minute. Now pressure cook for five minutes.
- When pressure is reduced, stir thoroughly. Add 4 tsp lemon juice and mix well.
- Put this in a serving dish. Garnish with onion rings, green chillies and coriander leaves.
- Serve hot with *tandoori roti*.

RAVA UTTAPAM

Ingredients
2 cups *suji* (semolina)
½ cup curd made from skimmed milk
½ tsp soda bi-carb
½ tsp salt
2 tsp chopped onion
¼ tsp crushed garlic
2 chopped green chillies
1 onion cut into two halves
Chopped coriander leaves
Oil for cooking

• *Servings 6 persons* • *Preparation time 10 mins. + standing time* • *Cooking time 20 mins.*
Per Serving *Protein (gms) 5* • *Fat (gms) 4* • *Fibre (gms) .6* • *Calories 150*

- Sieve *suji*, salt and soda bi-carb together. Mix curd and add water as required to make a fine batter, like fresh custard.
- Keep aside for 30 minutes. Then add finely chopped onion, green chillies and crushed garlic. Mix thoroughly.
- Put a little oil on the *tava* (griddle). Rub the onion-half all over it to make it slippery smooth.
- Pour half a cup of the batter. Spread it with a flat *katori*.
- Sprinkle some chopped onion and coriander leaves. Cook on medium flame till it is set.
- Flip it over on to the other side. Sprinkle a little oil and again cook till lightly golden brown on both the sides.
- Serve hot with coconut chutney or tomato chutney.

Ingredients
3 tsp olive oil
½ tsp crushed garlic
1 chopped spring onion
½ tsp red chilli powder
1 capsicum chopped into ½" square pieces
1 carrot diced into small pieces
100 gms mushrooms chopped
150 gms broccoli chopped into small bits
100 gms tofu (bean curd) or *paneer* made from skimmed milk
2 finely chopped tomatoes
2 tsp tomato ketchup
1 tsp honey
Salt to taste (1 tsp)

RARA VEGETABLES

• Servings 6 persons • Preparation time 0 mins. • Cooking time 0 mins.
Per Serving Protein (gms) 8 • Fat (gms) 4 • Fibre (gms) 7 • Calories 150

- Heat oil, add crushed garlic. Stir it and add onion and cook for two minutes.
- Add red chilli powder. Mix well and add capsicum, carrot, mushrooms, broccoli and chopped tomatoes.
- Sauté for two minutes. Cover and cook on slow fire for four minutes.
- Remove the lid. Add salt, honey, tomato ketchup and tofu or *paneer.* Sauté for two minutes.
- Garnish with coriander leaves. Serve hot with toasted wheat or brown bread or steamed brown rice.

SEMOLINA DHOKLA

Ingredients
250 gms *suji* (semolina)
1 level tsp salt
½ tsp turmeric powder
1½ tsp sugar
1 cup beaten curd made from skimmed milk
½ tsp soda bi-carb
2 finely chopped green chillies
1 tsp fruit salt (Eno)
Water as required

Contd.

• *Servings 6 persons* • *Preparation time 20 mins.* • *Cooking time 20 mins.*
Per Serving *Protein (gms) 5.8* • *Fat (gms) 1.4* • *Fibre (gms) .2* • *Calories 170*

- Sieve *suji*, salt, soda bi-carb and turmeric powder together.
- Add sugar and *hing*. Mix beaten curd in it. Add water as required and make a thick paste like custard. Mix green chillies.
- Boil water in the *dhokla*-maker or pressure cooker. Grease a plate (small *thali*).
- Add Eno in *dhokla* mixture and thoroughly beat it. Pour the mixture in the greased *thali* and place it on the stand in water. Cover it with a lid.
- Cook *dhokla* in steam for 15 minutes till set. Check that the knife comes out clean when inserted in it.
- Carefully remove the prepared *dhokla* and cut into 2" square pieces. Now pour *tadka* (tempering) on it to make it juicy.

Contd.

A pinch of *hing* (asafoetida)
Tempering
2 tsp oil
½ tsp mustard seeds
½ tsp *kalonji* (onion seeds)
3 tsp lemon juice or tamarind pulp
3 tsp sugar
2 cups of water
A pinch of *hing* (asafoetida)
A pinch of salt

TEMPERING

- Heat oil, add *hing*, mustard seeds and *kalonji*. Cook till they crackle.
- Add water, lemon juice, salt and sugar.
- Boil for a minute and immediately pour *tadka* on dhokla pieces.

Ingredients
250 gms *channa* (chickpeas)
1 tsp oil
½ tsp crushed garlic
1 tsp grated ginger
1 sliced onion
2 chopped green chillies
4 tsp chopped coriander leaves
½ tsp *garam masala*
½ tsp *kasuri methi*
1 tsp coriander powder
½ tsp red chilli powder
½ tsp roasted ground *jeera* (cumin seeds)

Contd.

CHICKPEA DELIGHT

• *Servings 6 persons* • *Preparation time 20 mins. + soaking time* • *Cooking time 30 mins.*
Per Serving *Protein (gms) 18* • *Fat (gms) 3* • *Fibre (gms) 9* • *Calories 200*

- Wash *channa* (chickpeas) and soak overnight in five cups of water, half tsp salt and a pinch of soda bi-carb (*meetha soda*).
- Pressure cook it in the same water in which it was soaked till tender (approximately five minutes as it begins to whistle).
- When pressure is reduced, separate water and keep aside.
- Mix salt, red chilli powder, coriander powder, *garam masala*, *kasuri methi*, roasted ground *jeera*, sugar and *saunf* to the boiled *channa*.
- In a *karahi* pour half of the separated water. Cook on high flame till it boils.
- Add *masala* mixed *channa* into it, while stirring. Cook till almost dry.

Contd.

½ tsp ground *saunf* (aniseed)
½ tsp sugar + ½ tsp salt
4 tsp thick tamarind pulp
1 boiled potato chopped into 1" cubes
A pinch of soda bi-carb

- Add potatoes, ginger, garlic, green chillies and coriander leaves.
- Mix and add rest of the water till almost dry. Mix tamarind pulp and remove from fire.
- Heat oil, add a pinch of *garam masala* and pour it on the cooked *channa*.
- Thoroughly mix them. Garnish with sliced onion, tomatoes and coriander leaves.
- Eat it hot or cold as *chaat*. Serve with *tandoori roti* or *kulcha*.

BROCCOLI & CORN SOUP

Vegetable Stalk
6 cups of water
2 cloves
½ tsp crushed garlic
1 finely chopped onion
½ tsp salt

Ingredients
1 cup broccoli chopped into small florets
1 cup cooked corn
½ cup thinly sliced carrots
½ cup finely chopped cabbage or lettuce leaves
1 blanched and chopped tomato
½ cup chopped tofu or *paneer* made from skimmed milk
½ tsp sugar
½ tsp black pepper
½ tsp salt
Chopped coriander leaves

- *Servings 6 (Bowls) persons* • *Preparation time 20 mins.* • *Cooking time 15 mins.*

Per Serving *Protein (gms) 1.4* • *Fat (gms) .2* • *Fibre (gms) .8* • *Calories 40*

- Boil all the ingredients of Vegetable Stalk for six minutes. Blend well and pass through a sieve. Reserve the stalk.
- Boil the prepared stalk. Add broccoli, corn, carrots and blanched and chopped tomatoe.
- Boil them for four minutes. Add salt, pepper and sugar. Cook for a minute.
- Add lettuce leaves or cabbage leaves, tofu or *paneer* and coriander leaves. Cook for a minute.
- Pour the soup in serving bowls. Serve hot with soup sticks or dinner rolls.

NAWABI KHUMB (MUSHROOM)

Ingredients
400 gms *khumbi* (mushrooms)
1 cup curd made from skimmed milk
1 tsp salt
½ tsp red chilli powder
1½ tsp coriander powder
1½ tsp grated ginger
A pinch of orange colour
2 or 3 tsp olive oil or double refined oil
½ tsp crushed garlic
4 or 5 crushed cardamoms
5 cloves

Contd.

- *Servings 6 persons*
- *Preparation time 10 mins. + 30 mins. marination*
- *Cooking time 15 mins.*

Per Serving *Protein (gms) 5 • Fat (gms) 3 • Fibre (gms) 3 • Calories 80*

- Wash mushrooms and drain the water. Wipe them. Lightly prick them.
- Marinate them with salt, red chilli powder, coriander powder, ginger, garlic, curd and orange colour. Cover and keep aside for 30 minutes.
- Heat oil in a pan. Add cloves, cardamoms and crushed garlic.
- Cook for half a minute. Add ½ tsp chilli powder, *garam masala* and *kasuri methi.*
- Stir and add marinated mushrooms. Cook on high flame for two minutes.
- Cover and cook on slow fire for two minutes. Remove the lid and cook till dry.

Contd.

½ tsp *kasuri methi*
½ tsp *garam masala*
½ tsp sugar
4 tsp chopped coriander leaves

- Add sugar and half cup water. Again cook on high flame till almost dry.
- Sprinkle lemon juice. Serve hot with onion rings. Garnish with coriander leaves.

CORN & VEGETABLES IN WHITE SAUCE

• Servings 6 persons • Preparation time 15 mins. • Cooking time 10 mins. + 5 mins. baking time

Per Serving Protein (gms) 20 • Fat (gms) 3.5 • Fibre (gms) 8 • Calories 150

Ingredients

2 cups corn kernels (cooked corn)
½ cup blanched and chopped spinach
1 carrot chopped into bits
½ cup chopped mushrooms
½ cup boiled peas
1 tsp olive oil
½ tsp crushed garlic
1 finely chopped onion
¼ tsp white or black pepper
4 tsp tomato ketchup
1 cup white sauce
2 crushed Monaco biscuits
4 tsp cornflakes crushed

Contd.

WHITE SAUCE

- Blend together cornflour, milk, salt, cloves and olive oil.
- Cook the mixture on slow fire till it becomes thick like a sauce or fresh custard. Cool and keep it covered.
- In a separate pan, heat oil, and add garlic. Stir and add onion. Cook for half a minute.
- Add corn, carrot, spinach, mushrooms and peas. Sauté it for a minute.
- Cover and cook on slow fire for four minutes.
- Remove the lid and add 2 tsp tomato ketchup in it. Mix and cook for a minute.

Contd.

White Sauce
1 tsp olive oil
2 cloves
3 tsp cornflour
1 cup skimmed milk
A pinch of salt

- Arrange the vegetables in a serving dish. Pour the prepared white sauce on it.
- Garnish with rest of the tomato ketchup. Sprinkle crushed Monaco biscuits and crushed cornflakes.
- Bake in a pre-heated oven at 200°C till the mixture is golden brown on top.
- Serve hot with garlic wheat bread.

MASALA MATTAR (PEAS)

Ingredients
2 cups fresh peas
2 tsp oil
½ tsp red chilli powder
½ tsp crushed garlic
1 tsp grated ginger
1 finely chopped onion
1 tsp dry coriander powder
¼ tsp turmeric powder
½ tsp *kasuri methi*
½ tsp *garam masala*

Contd.

• *Servings 6 persons* • *Preparation time 20 mins.* • *Cooking time 20 mins.*
Per Serving *Protein (gms) 30* • *Fat (gms) 3* • *Fibre (gms) 6.4* • *Calories 190*

- Wash peas and blanch them in salted water (approximately 1½ cup of water and ¼ tsp salt). Pass it through a sieve and keep aside the water.
- Heat oil in a pan. Add ginger and garlic. Stir and add chopped onion.
- Cook for four minutes. Add chilli powder, coriander powder, turmeric powder, *garam masala* and *kasuri methi*.
- Mix and add half a cup water and cook for a minute.
- Add ground melon seeds. Mix and again add half cup water. Cook for a minute.
- Add blanched peas and mix well. Cover and cook on slow fire for five minutes.

Contd.

4 tsp ground melon seeds
4 chopped and churned tomatoes (tomato puree)
2 chopped green chillies
Salt to taste (1 tsp)
Chopped coriander leaves

- Remove the lid. Add tomato puree, green chillies and salt.
- Mix and cook on high flame till almost dry. Now add the reserved water.
- Cook till the gravy thickens. Garnish with coriander leaves. Serve hot with *missi roti*.

KABULI BAIGUN

Ingredients

8 medium size *baigun* (brinjal)
2 medium size boiled potatoes
2 or 3 tsp oil

Filling

1 tsp salt
½ tsp red chilli powder
1½ tsp coriander powder
½ tsp turmeric powder
½ tsp roasted ground *jeera* (cumin seeds)
½ tsp *amchur* (mango powder)
½ tsp *garam masala*
½ tsp coarsely ground *saunf* (aniseed)
2 tsp ground melon seeds
½ tsp sugar

• Servings 6 persons • Preparation time 15 mins. • Cooking time 15 mins.
Per Serving Protein (gms) 15 • Fat (gms) 3 • Fibre (gms) 8.5 • Calories 160

- Mix all the ingredients of filling and keep aside.
- Wash and wipe the *baigun* (brinjals), make a slit horizontally. Cut potatoes into four pieces and make a slit in each of them.
- Fill *baigun* and potatoes with the prepared filling. Reserve the left over filling.
- Heat oil and grease the pan. Add stuffed *baigun* and potatoes. Sauté these for two minutes.
- Cover and cook on slow fire for eight minutes. Change the side once.
- Add the left over filling. Mix it and cover and cook for four minutes.
- Serve hot and garnish with beaten curd, strips of ginger and coriander leaves.
- Serve with *roomali roti* or *tava chappati.*

MIXED FRUIT YOGHURT

Ingredients

2 cups yoghurt made from skimmed milk
2 pineapple slices
10 to 12 cherries
1 cup grapes
1 cup chopped papaya
1 medium size banana
2 tsp honey or castor sugar
1 tsp salt
¼ tsp black/white pepper
A few mint leaves
Any fruit essence
A few strawberries (optional)

• Servings 6 persons • Preparation time 15 mins. • Cooking time 0 mins.

Per Serving Protein (gms) 6 • Fat (gms) 0 • Fibre (gms) 2 • Calories 30

- Lightly beat yoghurt along with salt, pepper, honey and essence.
- Chop pineapple slices into small bits. Cut banana into thin round slices. Cut papaya into cubes.
- Chop strawberries into thin slices. Deseed the cherries.
- Add all the chopped fruits into beaten yoghurt. Mix thoroughly. Add grapes.
- Put the fruit yoghurt into the serving bowl. Garnish with mint leaves and a few chopped cherries.
- Serve it as an appetiser or in the main course with *khasta roti*.

Chickpea Delight ➢

Overleaf Broccoli & Corn Soup

ALL BEANS SALAD

Ingredients

1 cup finely chopped and boiled French beans
1 cup boiled kidney beans
1 cup boiled black-eyed beans (*Lobia*)
1 cup corn kernels (cooked corns)
1 finely chopped spring onion or white onion
2 chopped green chillies
4 tsp chopped coriander leaves
100 gms cottage cheese (*paneer*) made from skimmed milk, chopped into small cubes
50 gms chopped mozzarella cheese cubes

Contd.

• Servings 6 persons • Preparation time 10 mins. • Cooking time 0 mins.
Per Serving Protein (gms) 10 • Fat (gms) 2 • Fibre (gms) 8.5 • Calories 150

- Mix all the ingredients given for dressing and keep aside.
- In a big bowl, mix together beans, kidney beans, black-eyed beans.
- Add corn kernels, onions, cottage cheese and mozzarella cheese.
- Add green chillies and coriander leaves.
- Prepare dressing by adding together lemon juice, salt, honey, vinegar, olive oil, ketchup, oregano, galic and ginger.
- Add the prepared dressing to the beans and vegetables.
- Mix thoroughly.
- Put the prepared salad in a serving dish or bowl.

Contd.

Dressing
3 tsp lemon juice
1 tsp salt
1 tsp castor sugar or honey
4 tsp vinegar
2 tsp olive oil
3 tsp tomato ketchup
¼ tsp oregano
½ tsp garlic paste
½ tsp ginger paste

- Garnish with a few cottage cheese cubes.
- Serve with corn chips (Nachos).

Ingredients
2 cups vermicelli (*Sevain*)
2 tsp oil
½ tsp mustard seeds
¼ tsp *kalonji* (onion seeds)
1 chopped onion
2 spring curry leaves
1 small capsicum chopped into bits
½ cup blanched beans chopped into bits
½ cup blanched peas
1 small carrot chopped into bits
2 chopped green chillies
4 tsp chopped coriander leaves
3 or 4 tsp lemon juice
A pinch of sugar
Salt to taste (1 level tsp)
A pinch of asafoetida

VERMICELLI UPMA

• Servings 6 persons • Preparation time 10 mins. • Cooking time 15 mins.
Per Serving Protein (gms) 6.8 • Fat (gms) 3 • Fibre (gms) 1.9 • Calories 175

- Heat oil. Add onions, capsicum, carrot, beans and green chillies. Sauté these for four minutes. Keep aside.
- In a separate pan, heat 1 tsp oil. Add mustard seeds, *kalonji*, asafoetida and curry leaves.
- Cook till the mustard seeds crackle. Add vermicelli. Stir and cook for one minute.
- Add one cup water. Cook till it boils. Add salt, sugar and cooked vegetables.
- Cook on high flame for two minutes. Cover with a lid and cook for one minute. Remove the lid and stir thoroughly.
- Put this in a serving dish. Sprinkle lemon juice. Garnish with coriander leaves.
- Serve hot with tomato chutney or sweet tamarind chutney.

LENTIL & BEAN SOUP

Ingredients
½ cup (*rajma*) kidney beans
2 tsp *moong dal*
1 tsp *masoor dal* (split lentil)
1 tsp *arhar dal* (*toovar dal*)
6 cups of water
1 tsp salt
2 cloves
2 tsp oil or 1 tsp butter
2 tsp chopped onion
2 blanched and chopped tomatoes
1 small carrot chopped into bits
½ cup chopped spinach
2 or 3 beans chopped into bits
½ tsp sugar
Chopped coriander leaves

• *Servings 6 (bowls) persons* • *Preparation time 20 mins.* • *Cooking time 20 mins.*
Per Serving *Protein (gms) 3* • *Fat (gms) 3.9* • *Fibre (gms) 3* • *Calories 120*

- Soak *rajma* overnight. Pressure cook *rajma* and other washed *dal* with six cups of water and cloves for seven minutes (till *rajma* is tender).
- When pressure is reduced, thoroughly stir it. (Reserve a few boiled kidney beans).
- Blend rest of the lentils and beans. In a pan melt butter, add onion and cook for half a minute.
- Add puree of lentils (*dal*) and tomatoes. Cook till it boils. Add salt and sugar. Cook for a minute.
- Add carrot, beans and spinach and again cook for four minutes.
- Serve hot. Garnish with coriander leaves, grated *paneer* and the reserved kidney beans.

Ingredients

1 cup brown rice or Basmati rice
3 tsp olive oil or bran oil
½ tsp garlic paste
4 or 5 cloves
1 stick of cinnamon
1 roughly chopped onion
½ tsp red chilli powder
1 cup fresh tomato puree
½ cup beaten curd made from skimmed milk
1 tsp salt
½ tsp sugar
½ tsp oregano
4 tsp crushed cornflakes

Contd.

RICE WITH CRISPY VEGETABLES

• Servings 6 persons • Preparation time 20 mins. • Cooking time 15 mins.

Per Serving • Protein (gms) 9.7 • Fat (gms) 3 • Fibre (gms) 1.7 • Calories 180.5

- Boil rice and pass through a sieve to remove the starch and cool it.
- Heat 1 tsp oil. Add all the chopped vegetables. Sauté it for four minutes. Add salt, black pepper and again cook for a minute.
- In a separate pan heat 2 tsp oil. Add cloves, cinnamon and garlic. Cook for 30 seconds. Add chopped onion.
- Cook for four minutes. Add red chilli powder. Mix and add tomato puree and sugar. Cook till reduced to half.
- Add curd and cook for two minutes. Now add boiled rice and salt.
- Cook on high flame till properly mixed. Add Sautéd

Contd.

Vegetables
1 big carrot chopped into small strips
100 gms blanched beans
100 gms thin slices of mushrooms
100 gms broccoli chopped in small strip
1 Zuccinni
¼ tsp salt
A pinch of black pepper

vegetables and oregano. Cook on high flame for four minutes.

- Place the prepared rice and vegetables in a serving bowl.
- Sprinkle crushed cornflakes. Bake in a pre-heated oven at 200°C for five minutes.
- Sprinkle ketchup and garnish with coriander leaves.
- Serve hot with salsa and toasted brown garlic bread.

TANDOORI STUFFED PARANTHA

Ingredients
2 cups *aata* (wheat flour)
1 cup fine *suji* (semolina)
½ tsp salt
A pinch of sugar
Lukewarm water for kneading the dough

Filling
1 big *mooli* (radish) + 1 onion
1 tsp ginger
½ tsp *ajwain* (caraway seeds)
1 tsp *anardana*
2 finely chopped green chillies
1 tsp salt
¼ tsp turmeric powder
1 tsp oil
Chopped coriander leaves (2 tsp)
A few soft radish leaves

• *Servings 6 persons* • *Preparation time 25 mins.* • *Cooking time 20 mins.*
Per Serving *Protein (gms) 10.5* • *Fat (gms) 2* • *Fibre (gms) 3* • *Calories 180*

- Peel, wash and grate the radish. Add ¼ tsp salt and mix well. Now squeeze it.
- Heat 1 tsp oil in a pan. Add *ajwain*, ginger, onion and turmeric powder. Cook for half a minute.
- Add radish, green chillies, coriander leaves, radish leaves, *anardana* and salt.
- Mix thoroughly and again cook for half a minute. Cool the mixture.
- Make two lemon sized balls from the dough. Roll them into 6" *chappatis.* Spread the prepared filling on one *chappati.*
- Cover with the second *chappati*. Press the edges and seal it. Now lightly roll it to make it even.
- Cook in a pre-heated electric *tandoor* or clay oven, till *parantha* is crisp and golden brown.
- Serve hot with beaten curd and mint chutney.

Ingredients
2 medium size boiled potato slices
1 carrot chopped into thin slices
1 cup broccoli or cauliflower chopped into small florets
5 or 6 mushrooms chopped into thin slices
½ cup boiled peas
1 cup boiled pasta
2 tsp olive oil
½ tsp crushed garlic
2 tsp chopped onion
2 chopped green chillies
1 tsp salt
½ tsp white pepper
¼ tsp mustard powder
2 tsp lemon juice

Contd.

BAKED VEGETABLES

• *Servings 6 persons* • *Preparation time 30 mins.* • *Cooking time 10 mins. + 15 mins. baking time*

Per Serving *Protein (gms) 30* • *Fat (gms) 3* • *Fibre (gms) 8* • *Calories 180*

- Blend all the ingredients of cottage cheese sauce together till smooth.
- Heat oil in a pan. Add crushed garlic and onion. Cook for half a minute.
- Add sliced potatoes, carrot, broccoli, mushrooms and peas.
- Sauté for a minute, then cover and cook on slow fire for four minutes.
- Remove the lid and add salt, white pepper, mustard powder and green chillies. Cook for a minute.
- Mix lemon juice, honey and boiled pasta. Toss it thoroughly.
- Arrange the vegetables and boiled pasta in an oven-proof

Contd.

1 tsp honey
4 crushed Monaco biscuits

Cottage Cheese Sauce
100 gms *paneer* made from skimmed milk
1 cup skimmed milk
2 chopped green chillies
¼ tsp salt
1 tsp chopped coriander leaves

serving dish. Pour cottage cheese sauce over it. Sprinkle crushed Monaco biscuits on it.

- Bake in a pre-heated oven at 200°C for five minutes.
- Serve hot with toasted garlic bread or warm corn tortilla.

BEACH SALAD

• Servings 6 persons • Preparation time 30 mins. • Cooking time 0 mins.
Per Serving Protein (gms) 7 • Fat (gms) .5 • Fibre (gms) 3 • Calories 60

Ingredients

Dressing

- ½ cup thick beaten curd made from skimmed milk
- 1 tsp salt
- 2 chopped green chillies
- 1 tsp castor sugar
- 1 tsp lemon juice
- 4 tsp beetroot paste or ½ cup grated beetroot

Salad

- 1 thickly grated cucumber
- 1 boiled and grated potato
- 1 finely chopped onion
- 2 pineapple slices chopped into bits
- A few mint leaves

Contd.

- Mix all the ingredients of dressing till smooth.
- Keep grated cucumber in a colander so that the extra liquid separates out (don't squeeze it). Mix together potato, onion, pineapple, cucumber together.
- Add prepared dressing and mix thoroughly. Arrange the salad in an oval-shaped dish, so that the salad retains the shape of the dish, leaving a 1" boundary.

BOATS

- Peel potatoes, cut them lengthwise. Now scoop out the potatoes, leaving ½" boundary. It should retain the shape of the potato.
- Sprinkle salt, red pepper and lemon juice on potato cases.

Contd.

Boat

2 medium size boiled potatoes
½ cup thick hung curd made from skimmed milk
2 tsp chopped onion
1 chopped green chilli
¼ tsp salt, ¼ tsp red pepper
1 broad piece of carrot in thin broad slices
A few mint leaves chopped fine

- Mash scooped out potato. Add onion, green chillies, mint leaves, hung curd and salt. Mix thoroughly.
- Fill the potato cases with the prepared mixture. Now cut the carrot slices into triangles.
- Arrange them lengthwise on stuffed potato cases to give a look of the boat.
- Arrange potato boats all around the beach salad.
- Garnish the salad with thin, round carrot slices and mint leaves.

SWEET & SOUR SALAD

Ingredients (Dressing)

½ cup mint chutney
½ cup tomato ketchup
½ cup low fat cream or hung curd made from skimmed milk
1 tsp salt
2 chopped green chillies
2 tsp lemon juice
2 tsp honey

Salad

2 finely chopped spring onion or white onion
1 cup boiled peas
1 cup halved green grapes
1 apple chopped into small cubes
2 medium size boiled potatoes chopped into small cubes
2 tomatoes chopped into bits
1 cucumber chopped into bits

• *Servings 6 persons* • *Preparation time 20 mins.* • *Cooking time 0 mins.*

Per Serving *Protein (gms) 8* • *Fat (gms) 0* • *Fibre (gms) 5.8* • *Calories 60*

- Mix all the ingredients of dressing till smooth.
- In a large bowl put all the fruits and vegetables.
- Add the prepared dressing. Mix thoroughly till the dressing is coated on all the fruits and vegetables.
- Arrange the salad in a serving dish.
- Garnish with grated *paneer* and chopped mint leaves.

Ingredients
200 gms medium size boiled pasta
1 spring onion finely chopped with green crisp part
1 small green, red and yellow bell pepper or 1 large capsicum chopped into small strips
100 gms par-boiled mushrooms
1 cup cooked corn kernels
1 cup small florets of broccolli (blanched)
1 cup roasted walnuts
Lettuce leaves (1 bunch)

Contd.

ITALIAN PASTA SALAD

• *Servings 6 persons* • *Preparation time 20 mins.* • *Cooking time 15 mins. for boiling pasta.*

Per Serving *Protein (gms) 15 • Fat (gms) 3 • Fibre (gms) 4 • Calories 180*

- Put all the ingredients of dressing in a bottle or a cocktail-shaker. Shake thoroughly or blend all the ingredients.
- In a large bowl, put together the boiled pasta, small strips of bellpeppers, mushroom, corn, broccoli, walnuts, spring onion and lettuce leaves.
- Add the prepared dressing and mix thoroughly so that the dressing is coated on the pasta and vegetables.
- Place this in a serving bowl. Cover with a thin film of aluminium foil and refrigerate for 30 minutes.

HOW TO BOIL PASTA

- Boil water along with ½ tsp oil.

Contd.

Dressing
3 tsp olive oil
6 tsp vinegar
3 tsp lemon juice
½ tsp crushed garlic
2 tsp coriander leaves
2 tsp castor sugar
½ tsp oregano
2 tsp tomato ketchup

- Add pasta and cook for 8 to 10 minutes, stirring all the while. Keep in the same water for four or five minutes.
- Pass it through a sieve and pass through fresh water. (It should be firm to bite). For any small shape, boil for four or five minutes.
- Lettuce leaves should be kept in chilled water so that they remain crisp. Do not cut, but tear them with hands.
- You can make the dressing by one or two days in advance.

CRUNCHY BAKED CUTLETS

Ingredients

1 cup fine *suji* (semolina)
3 tsp olive oil or low fat butter
1 cup skimmed milk
½ cup water
2 chopped green chillies
4 tsp chopped onion
½ tsp salt
100 gms *paneer* made from skimmed milk
1 tsp roasted and ground *jeera*
½ cup desiccated coconut
1 tsp grated ginger
2 chopped curry leaves
2 tsp chopped coriander leaves
4 tsp bread crumbs
½ cup crushed cornflakes

Contd.

• *Servings 12 persons* • *Preparation time 30 mins.* • *Baking time 8 mins.*

Per Serving *Protein (gms) 8.8* • *Fat (gms) 2* • *Fibre (gms) 1.8* • *Calories 200*

- Heat oil or melt butter; add onion and green chillies. Cook for half a minute.
- Add *suji*. Roast it for three or four minutes. Remove from fire.
- Add milk, mix thoroughly. Add water and salt. Cook on medium flame till thick and non-dripping.
- Remove from fire and refrigerate for 30 minutes.
- In a large bowl mix together the *suji* cooked dough. Grated *paneer*, onion, green chillies, ginger, desiccated coconut, curry leaves, coriander leaves, roasted ground *jeera* and salt. Mix thoroughly till smooth like a dough.
- With wet hands take a small portion of the dough. Make a round ball and flatten it to make a round cutlet.

Contd.

Dhaba Salad
2 medium size onions, cut into thin round slices
¼ tsp salt
¼ tsp red chilli powder
2 tsp coriander leaves
3 tsp lemon juice

- Coat it with crushed cornflakes and bread crumbs. Similarly make all the cutlets.
- Grease a baking dish. Arrange the cutlets. Sprinkle 1 tsp oil on them.
- Bake in a pre-heated oven at 220°C for eight minutes till golden brown.
- Serve hot with Dhaba salad and coconut chutney or tomato chutney.

DHABA SALAD

Mix all the ingredients for the Dhaba salad and serve.

Mixed Fruit Yoghurt ➢

Overleaf Broccoli & Baby Corn Jalferezi

CORN ENCHILADAS

Ingredients

8 corn tortillas (Mexican bread)
1 cup Mexican tomato sauce
1 bowl of corn and cottage cheese filling
Mozzarella cheese as required or ½ tsp grated (optional) for each Enchiladas

Contd.

• *Servings 8 persons* • *Preparation time 30 mins.* • *Cooking time 10 mins. + baking time*
Per Serving Protein (gms) 4 • *Fat (gms) 2* • *Fibre (gms) 8* • *Calories 180*

- Spread 2 or 3 tsp of Mexican tomato sauce on each tortilla.
- Put 4 tsp of the corn and cottage cheese filling in them. Roll them.
- Arrange them in a greased baking tray (seamy side down).
- Moist them with Mexican tomato sauce. Sprinkle ½ tsp of mozzarella cheese on each. Bake in a pre-heated oven at 200°C till the cheese bubbles.
- Serve hot with crisp lettuce leaves, salsa and cooked lentils (instead of making corn enchiladas, you can make flour enchiladas).
- Procedure is same. Instead of maize flour, use refined flour (*maida*).

Contd.

Ingredients
1 cup *aata* (wheat flour)
1 cup *makai ka aata* (maize flour)
½ tsp salt
1 tsp oil
Lukewarm water for kneading the dough

Filling
1 cup corn kernels
1 finely chopped onion
1 cup grated cottage cheese made from skimmed milk
1 tomato chopped into bits
1 or 2 green chillies
2 tsp chopped coriander leaves
1 tsp olive oil
½ tsp crushed garlic
½ tsp salt
½ tsp oregano

Contd.

CORN TORTILLA

- Sieve *aata*, *makai ka aata* and salt together. Add oil and mix it.
- Gradually add lukewarm water to make a soft and smooth dough.
- Cover with a wet napkin and keep for half an hour. Then knead again for two minutes.
- Roll 6" *chappati* and lightly cook on a pre-heated oven on both sides. Cover each with a dry napkin.

FILLING

- Heat oil, add garlic. Stir and add green chillies and onion.
- Cook for two minutes. Add corn kernels, salt and oregano.
- Sauté for two minutes. Then mix chopped tomatoes and cottage cheese.
- Again cook for a minute. Remove from fire and add coriander leaves.

Contd.

Mexican Tomato Sauce

5 or 6 blanched and chopped tomatoes
1 tsp olive oil
½ tsp crushed garlic
½ level tsp red chilli powder
¼ tsp oregano
½ tsp salt
½ tsp sugar
½ tsp vinegar

MEXICAN TOMATO SAUCE

- Heat oil, add garlic, stir and add red chilli powder and oregano. Mix and add blanched and chopped tomatoes. Cook for four minutes.
- Add salt, sugar and vinegar and again cook for a minute.
- Cool it and churn or blend it. You can make this sauce a day in advance.

CRISPY CRUNCHY MEAL

Ingredients
1 cup sprouted *moong dal*
1 finely chopped onion
½ tsp crushed garlic
2 or 3 green chillies
4 tsp chopped coriander leaves
2 chopped tomatoes
1 boiled potato chopped (optional)
1 capsicum chopped into small strips
2 tsp olive oil or bran oil
½ tsp red chilli powder
¼ tsp turmeric powder
1 tsp coriander powder
1 tsp roasted ground *jeera* (cumin seeds)
3 tsp lemon juice
A pinch of sugar + 1 tsp salt
A few ginger strips

• *Servings 6 persons* • *Preparation time 15 mins.* • *Cooking time 15 mins.*
Per Serving Protein (gms) 25 • *Fat (gms) 3* • *Fibre (gms) 9* • *Calories 175*

- Heat oil, add garlic. Stir and add onion. Cook for two minutes.
- Add red chilli powder, turmeric powder and coriander powder.
- Mix in half cup of water. Cook for a minute. Add sprouted *moong dal*, capsicum, potato, tomatoes, salt and sugar. Sauté for one minute.
- Then cover and cook on slow fire for two minutes. Remove the lid.
- Add green chillies, ginger strips and coriander leaves.
- Sprinkle lemon juice and *jeera*. Serve hot with *chappatis* or as it is.

Ingredients

1 cup wheat flakes
2 tsp roasted *suji* (semolina)
300 ml skimmed milk (1½ cup)
1 tsp honey
1 tsp strawberry crush
1 cup assorted fruits chopped into small cubes—strawberries, cherries, apples, grapes and papaya, etc.
A few raisins
A few pistachios (optional)

MORNING GLORY

• *Servings 4 persons* • *Preparation time 10 mins.* • *Cooking time 7 mins.*

Per Serving *Protein (gms) 15* • *Fat (gms) 3* • *Fibre (gms) 4.5* • *Calories 180*

- Mix *suji* and milk. Boil till thick. Remove from fire and add honey. Cool and refrigerate it.
- In a broad bowl, put the chopped fruits, raisins and wheat flakes. Pour chilled thick *suji* and milk mixture on them. Sprinkle strawberry crush.
- Garnish with flaked pistachios. This is a healthy and nutritious breakfast with less calories.

RAINBOW IDLIS (INSTANT IDLIS)

Ingredients
½ kg *suji* (semolina)
1 tsp salt
1 cup curd made from skimmed milk
½ tsp soda bi-carb
1 tsp Eno fruit salt
½ tsp roasted mustard seeds
2 chopped curry leaves
4 tsp beetroot paste

Contd.

• *Servings 24 persons* • *Preparation time 20 mins.* • *Cooking time 20 mins. + 5 mins. for tempering*

Per Serving *Protein (gms) 5.6* • *Fat (gms) 2* • *Fibre (gms) .5* • *Calories 150*

- Sieve *suji*, salt and soda bi-carb together.
- Add curd. Lightly mix it. Add water as required and make a thick paste like custard.
- Keep covered for 30 minutes. Then add Eno fruit salt. Thoroughly mix it.
- Divide the mixture into three parts. In the first part mix beetroot paste till properly mixed to get red colour.
- In the second portion mix turmeric powder to get yellow colour.
- In the third portion add mint chutney and two drops of green colour. Mix thoroughly.

Contd.

½ tsp turmeric powder
2 tsp mint chutney
2 drops of green colour
Water as required

- Boil water in *idli*-maker or pressure cooker. Grease *idli* mould. Pour 4 tsp of red mixture, 4 tsp of green mixture, 4 tsp of yellow mixture in each *idli* mould.
- Steam the *idlis* for 10 to 15 minutes till the knife comes out smoothly.
- Sprinkle water and take out the *idlis*.
- Season on top with tempering (Heat oil; add curry leaves and mustard seeds, cook till the seeds splutter).
- Serve hot with tomato chutney and coconut chutney (*sambhar* if desired).

WHOLESOME ROTI

Ingredients
1 cup *aata* (wheat flour)
1 cup soyabean flour
1 cup *besan* (black gram flour)
½ tsp salt
½ tsp *ajwain* (caraway seeds)
1 tsp oil
Chopped coriander leaves
Lukewarm water for kneading the dough

• Servings 6 persons • Preparation time 15 mins. • Cooking time 25 mins.
Per Serving Protein (gms) 12 • Fat (gms) .5 • Fibre (gms) 4 • Calories 160

- Sieve *aata*, soyabean flour, *besan* and salt together, so that these are properly mixed. Don't throw the *chokar* (remains of *aata*).
- Again mix it in the sieved flours. Add salt, *ajwain* and oil. Lightly mix and add coriander leaves.
- Gradually add water and make a soft and smooth dough.
- Keep covered with a wet napkin for 15 minutes. Again knead it for two minutes to remove the air bubbles.
- Make 6"-diameter *chappati* (slightly thicker than normal *chappati*).
- Cook on a pre-heated greased *tava* (griddle) till lightly golden brown on both sides.
- Serve hot with beaten curd (made from low-fat milk) and onion slices.

TAMARIND DRINK

Ingredients
50 gm seedless tamarind
1 cup boiled water
1 tsp salt
2 tsp castor sugar
½ tsp black salt
1 tsp roasted ground *jeera* (cumin seeds)
1 tsp lemon juice
2 tsp chopped mint leaves
4 tsp coriander leaves
¼ tsp cardamom powder
¼ tsp ground *saunf* (aniseed)
6 cups of water
Crushed ice as required

• *Servings 6 persons* • *Preparation time 30 mins. + soaking time* • *Cooking time 0 mins.*
Per Serving • *Protein (gms) .5* • *Fat (gms) 0* • *Fibre (gms) 1* • *Calories 20*

- Soak tamarind in a cup of boiled water for half an hour. Mix or blend it.
- Press through a sieve and extract the pulp.
- Add six cups of water. Mix well. Add salt, roasted ground *jeera*, sugar, cardamom powder, *saunf*, black salt, mint leaves and lemon juice.
- Mix thoroughly or blend well. Add crushed ice and coriander leaves.
- Pour in individual glasses and garnish with lemon wedge and spring mint.

KESAR-GULAB DELIGHT

Ingredients for 5 glasses
1 litre skimmed milk
¼ tsp cardamom powder
¼ tsp *kesar* (saffron)
4 tsp honey
1 tsp *gulab jal* (rosewater)
1 tsp low-fat almond powder
A few rose petals

• Servings 5 persons • Preparation time 5 mins. • Cooking time 10 mins.
Per Serving Protein (gms) 4 • Fat (gms) 1.5 • Fibre (gms) .5 • Calories 180

- Boil milk along with cardamom powder and *kesar*.
- Cook on slow fire for five minutes. Add almond powder and again cook for a minute. Remove from fire.
- Add honey and *gulab jal*. Chill in the refrigerator.
- Pour the drink in glasses and garnish with rose petals.
- This is a healthy drink for those who want to reduce weight.

LEMON ROCK FROST

Ingredients
2 tsp tamarind pulp
2 tsp sugar syrup
¼ tsp black rock salt
1 tsp fresh lemon juice
¼ tsp salt
¼ tsp black pepper
1 lemon wedge
A few rose petals
Chopped coriander leaves
A handful of crushed ice or
 4 ice cubes
Any aerated lemon drink
Chopped mint leaves

• *Servings 1 (glass) persons* • *Preparation time 4 mins.* • *Cooking time 0 mins.*
Per Serving *Protein (gms) 1* • *Fat (gms) 0* • *Fibre (gms) .5* • *Calories 80*

- In a tall broad glass, pour the tamarind pulp. Add sugar syrup, black rock salt, lemon juice, salt, chopped mint leaves, black pepper and coriander leaves. Stir well.
- Add crushed ice and top with an aerated drink like Limca or Sprite.
- Arrange one lemon wedge on each glass. Garnish with rose-petals.

MANNA-COLADA

Ingredients
4 tsp raw mango pulp
1 tsp sugar syrup
6 tsp coconut milk
150 ml any lemon drink (Sprite, Limca)
3 or 4 cherries
A few lemon wedges
A few mint leaves
Some crushed ice

• *Servings 1 (glass) persons* • *Preparation time 5 mins.* • *Cooking time 0 mins.*
Per Serving *Protein (gms) 2* • *Fat (gms) .1* • *Fibre (gms) .4* • *Calories 50*

- In a tall glass pour the mango pulp and sugar syrup. Stir well. Top the glass with two cherries.
- Add coconut milk. Lightly stir it.
- Add crushed ice and top it with Limca, Sprite or 7-Up.
- Arrange the lemon wedge and two cherries on each glass. Garnish with mint leaves.

FRUITY DROPLETS

Ingredients
1 cup chopped apple
1 cup chopped papaya
1 cup grapes
5 or 6 strawberries or raspberries
1 cup fresh pomegranate seeds or chopped pineapple
2 or 3 tsp honey
1 tsp lemon juice
4 tsp cornflour
½ tsp any fruit essence
1 cup assorted chopped fruits
½ cup desiccated coconut
2 drops green colour
2 drops red colour

• *Servings 6 persons* • *Preparation time 10 mins.* • *Cooking time 15 mins. + freezing time*
Per Serving *Protein (gms) 3* • *Fat (gms) 2* • *Fibre (gms) 4.5* • *Calories 100*

- Blend together apple, papaya, grapes, strawberry and pomegranate seeds till smooth.
- Add honey and lemon juice. Mix thoroughly.
- Mix cornflour to the prepared paste and cook on a medium flame till very thick. Remove from fire.
- Cool it and add fruit essence and the assorted, chopped fruits. Keep in the freezing chamber till set.
- Divide desiccated coconut into two parts. To one part add two drops of red colour and mix well. To second part mix green colour.
- Garnish with red and green coconut in whirls. Serve chilled.

STRAWBERRY FRUIT DELIGHT

Ingredients

1 bowl of chopped assorted fruits, five or six fruits of your choice, except guava, water melon, papaya
1 cup grapes
½ cup fresh pomegranate seeds
1 peeled and chopped apple
1 peeled and chopped orange
6 strawberries
6 raspberries
2 kiwi fruits
2 chopped pineapple slices
1 packet of strawberry jelly crystals
2 cups of hot water
1 tsp lemon juice
1 tsp honey
½ tsp strawberry essence

• *Servings 6 persons* • *Preparation time 15 mins.* • *Cooking time 2 mins. + chilling time 1 hour*

Per Serving *Protein (gms) 3 • Fat (gms) .5 • Fibre (gms) 2.5 • Calories 90*

- In a large bowl keep the assorted fruits. Add lemon juice, honey and strawberry essence. Mix thoroughly.
- In a separate bowl mix jelly crystals in hot water till completely dissolved.
- Keep in the freezing chamber for 10 minutes till a little thick.
- Add chopped fruits. Now in any shape of rinsed jelly mould, pour the fruits and jelly mixture.
- Keep it in the freezing chamber till set and firm.
- Unmould it in the serving dish. Decorate with low-fat whipped cream.
- Arrange some cherries and mint leaves on top.

CORN & BUTTON MUSHROOMS

Ingredients
200 gms button mushrooms
1 cup corn kernels
2 chopped spring onions
1 capsicum (chopped into strips)
8-10 spinach leaves, torn
3 tsp refined oil
1 tsp crushed garlic
½ tsp red pepper
1 tsp soya sauce
2 tsp chilli sauce
1 tsp vinegar
1 tsp honey
4 tsp cornflour
300 ml (1½ cup) water
1 tsp salt

• Servings 6 persons • Preparation time 10 mins. • Cooking time 20 mins.
Per Serving Protein (gms) 6 • Fat (gms) 3 • Fibre (gms) 4 • Calories 100

- Heat oil, add garlic, stir it and add onions. Cook for a minute.
- Add mushrooms, corn and capsicum. Stir it. Cover and cook on slow fire for two minutes. Remove the lid, add red pepper and mix thoroughly.
- Add soya sauce, chilli sauce, vinegar and honey. Mix them.
- Mix cornflour with water till smooth.
- Add to the mushrooms. Cook till it boils.
- Add salt and spinach leaves. Cook on slow fire till the sauce thickens.
- Serve hot with steamed rice.

Ingredients
1 cup *maida* (refined flour)
2 tsp oil + ½ tsp salt
Lukewarm water for dough
Corn Filling
1 cup corn kernels (cooked corn)
½ cup finely chopped carrot
½ cup finely chopped cabbage
1 spring onion or white onion (finely chopped)
½ cup cottage cheese made from skimmed milk or tofu (chopped into small bits)
½ tsp salt to taste
¼ tsp black pepper
1 green chilli chopped
2 tsp coriander leaves
1 tsp oil
½ tsp grated ginger
2 garlic cloves, crushed

CORNISH DIMSUM

• *Servings 18 pieces (6) persons* • *Preparation time 30 mins.* • *Cooking time 20 mins*
Per Serving *Protein (gms) 3* • *Fat (gms) .5* • *Fibre (gms) 2.9* • *Calories 70*

FILLING

- Heat oil in a pan, add ginger and garlic. Stir it and add rest of the ingredients. Stir it and remove from fire. Cool it.

DOUGH

- Sieve *maida* and salt together. Add oil and mix it. Now gradually add water. Make a smooth and slightly firm dough.
- Make small balls out of the dough and roll 4"-diameter thin *chappatis*. Put 2 tsp of filling in each *chappati*.
- Half fold it and join the edges. Make notches in each.
- Grease the steamer and arrange the dimsum pieces in it. Steam for 10 minutes. Serve hot with red hot chilli garlic sauce.

Oat & Date Muffins ➤

Overleaf Cocktail-Fruit Sticks

VEGETABLES IN CHANNA DAL

Ingredients
1 cup *Channa dal*
6 cups water
1 tsp salt + ½ tsp turmeric
½ tsp red chilli powder
1 cup peas (blanched)
100 gms beans (blanched)
1 chopped carrot
1 cup broccoli (chopped into small florets)
10 gms cottage cheese made from skimmed milk, chopped into bits
2 tomatoes, finely chopped
2 green chillies, finely chopped
1 tsp lemon juice
3 tsp oil + a pinch of sugar
½ tsp *jeera* (cumin seeds)
½ tsp *garam masala*
Chopped coriander leaves

• Servings 6 persons • Preparation time 15 mins. • Cooking time 25-30 mins.
Per Serving Protein (gms) 18 • Fat (gms) 1 • Fibre (gms) 10 • Calories 140

- Wash *channa dal* and soak for 15 minutes.
- Pressure cook it in six cups of water, salt, red chilli powder and turmeric powder for six minutes on high flame.
- When pressure is reduced, thoroughly mix it.
- Add peas, beans, carrot and broccolli. Cook on high flame for five minutes, stirring in between.
- Add tomatoes, cottage cheese, green chillies and half of the coriander leaves.
- Cook for a minute. Mix lemon juice and sugar and remove from fire.
- Heat oil, add *jeera* and cook till it crackles. Add *garam masala* and pour over the *dal*.
- Garnish with onion rings and rest of the coriander leaves. Serve hot with *methi ki roti* or spinach *roti.*

MUSHROOMS WITH JALAPENOS

Ingredients
400 gms button mushrooms
3 tsp olive oil
½ tsp crushed garlic
2 spring onions or white onion roughly chopped
2 tomatoes chopped into bits
½ cup deseeded olives
3 tsp Jalapenos chillies
1 tsp salt
½ tsp brown sugar
½ tsp oregano
20 gms cottage cheese made from skimmed milk
Chopped coriander leaves

• Servings 6 persons • Preparation time 10 mins. • Cooking time 15 mins.
Per Serving Protein (gms) 2.8 • Fat (gms) 2 • Fibre (gms) 3.5 • Calories 40

- Heat oil. Add mushrooms, onion and garlic.
- Cook it on high flame for six minutes till mushrooms are dry and thoroughly cooked.
- Add tomatoes, brown sugar, olives, jalapenos and salt. Cook till dry. Remove from fire.
- Add oregano and mix thoroughly. Place it in a serving bowl.
- Garnish with coriander leaves and grated cottage cheese.
- Serve hot with wheat bread or bran bread.

Ingredients
10 baby potatoes (boiled)
1 cup mint leaves
¼ cup roasted peanuts
3 tsp oil
¼ tsp mustard seeds
¼ tsp *kalonji* (onion seeds)
¼ tsp *jeera* (cumin seeds)
2 green chillies, chopped
¼ tsp turmeric powder
1 tsp coriander powder
1 tsp salt
3 tsp beaten curd
A pinch of sugar
Two small onions

PUDINEWALE AALU

• *Servings 4 persons* • *Preparation time 10 mins.* • *Cooking time 15 mins.*
Per Serving *Protein (gms) 3* • *Fat (gms) 2* • *Fibre (gms) 3* • *Calories 40*

- Peel potatoes, prick them and keep aside. Chop mint leaves.
- Heat oil in a pan, add mustard seeds, *kalonji* and *jeera*. Cook till they crackle.
- Add onions, peanuts and chillies and cook for two minutes.
- Add turmeric and coriander powder, stir and add potatoes.
- Sauté it for four minutes. Add beaten curd. Mix well.
- Add salt, sugar and mint leaves. Sauté it for four minutes.
- Serve hot with warm *chappati*.

THAI FLAT NOODLES

Ingredients

150 gms flat rice noodles (boiled and drained)
1 cup finally chopped broccoli
50 gms mushrooms chopped into thin slices
1 spring onion roughly chopped (with green crisp leaves)
1 small red chilli
1 green chilli (deseeded, chopped into thin strips)
1 garlic clove, crushed
2 tsp soya sauce
1 tsp honey
3 tsp oil
Salt to taste
Few ginger julienes (strips)

• Servings 6 persons • Preparation time 15 mins. • Cooking time 10 mins.

Per Serving Protein (gms) 4.5 • Fat (gms) 3 • Fibre (gms) 2.8 • Calories 140

- Heat oil in a wok. Add onions, ginger and garlic. Sauté for two minutes.
- Add broccoli, mushrooms, green chilli and red pepper. Cook for four minutes.
- Add soya sauce and ginger julienes. Stir well.
- Add rice noodles, salt, honey and cook it on high flame till properly mixed and cooked.
- Serve immediately.

BROCCOLI & BABYCORN JALFEREZI

Ingredients

200 gms broccoli, trimmed and chopped into small florets
12 baby corns, chopped
1 spring onion, chopped
1 carrot thinly chopped
1 capsicum chopped into small pieces
2 big tomatoes (finely chopped)
2 green chillies (sliced lengthwise)
2 tsp butter
½ tsp crushed garlic
1 tsp grated ginger
½ tsp red chilli powder
½ tsp roasted ground *jeera*
½ tsp *garam masala*
1 tsp salt

Contd.

- *Servings 6 persons* • *Preparation time 20 mins.* • *Cooking time 20 mins.*

Per Serving Protein (gms) 5 • Fat (gms) 6 • Fibre (gms) 5 • Calories 100

- Melt butter and add ginger and garlic to it. Stir well.
- Add onions and cook for two minutes.
- Add red chilli powder, mix it.
- Add broccoli, baby corns, carrots and capsicum.
- Stir and cover it to cook for two minutes.
- Remove the lid and add chopped tomatoes, green chillies and salt.
- Cook for a minute. Sprinkle *garam masala*, cover it and cook for two minutes.
- Add tomato ketchup and soya cream. Sauté this for two minutes.
- Put it in a serving dish. Sprinkle roasted and ground *jeera*.

Contd.

3 tsp tomato ketchup
2 tsp chopped coriander leaves
50 ml soya cream (optional)
Few ginger strips (julienes)

- Garnish with ginger julienes and chopped coriander leaves.
- Serve hot with *tandoori* onion *parantha* or *pudina parantha*.

OAT & DATE MUFFINS

Ingredients
1½ cup whole wheat flour
½ cup plain flour
1½ tsp baking powder
½ tsp soda bicarb
1 cup quick rolled oat (white oats)
½ cup soft brown sugar or castor sugar
1 cup chopped dates
½ tsp cinnamon powder
6 tsp vegetable oil or olive oil
4 tsp honey
1½ cup skimmed milk
1 egg or 3 tsp condensed milk

• Servings 12 persons • Preparation time 20 mins. • Baking time 20 mins.
Per Serving Protein (gms) 5 • Fat (gms) 3 • Fibre (gms) 2 • Calories 160

- Sieve together wheat flour, plain flour, baking powder, soda bicarb in a large bowl. Add the husk back into the above ingredients.
- Add oats and brown sugar, cinnamon powder and chopped dates.
- Beat together egg, oil, honey and skimmed milk. Gradually pour the milk mixture into the dry ingredients.
- Lightly mix them. Do not over-mix.
- Lightly grease the muffin moulds. Spoon the mixture into each mould.
- Bake at 150°C for 20 minutes till the muffins rise up and are lightly golden brown.
- Remove from the oven and cover them for five minutes.
- Unmould and serve with tea or coffee.

BAKED HASH BROWN

Ingredients
6 medium size parboiled potatoes
¼ tsp black pepper
½ tsp salt
2 or 3 tsp olive oil for cooking
A slice of onion

• Servings 6 persons • Preparation time 20 mins. • Cooking time 10 mins.
Per Serving Protein (gms) 2.5 • Fat (gms) 1 • Fibre (gms) 1.5 • Calories 65

- Boil potatoes, so that they are tender from outside but firm from within.
- Peel them and grate them thickly. Sprinkle salt and pepper over them
- Pre heat the oven at 200°C for seven minutes.
- Oil the baking tray.
- Rotate an onion slice all over the tray to make it smooth and slippery.
- Divide the mixture into six parts. With your wet hands take one portion of the potato and shape it into a flat, oval shaped patty.
- Arrange these patties on a pre-heated greased baking tray. Increase the temperature to 250°C. Bake for 10 minutes.

Contd.

- After five minutes, change the sides of the potatoes by flipping them over and bake till crisp and golden.
- Serve hot with yoghurt dip.

OAT, WHEAT & METHI PARANTHA

Ingredients
½ cup oat bran
½ cup wheat bran
½ cup normal flour
½ tsp salt
¼ tsp *ajwain* (caraway seeds)
1 tsp grated ginger
2 green chopped chillies
½ tsp ground *jeera* (ground cumin seeds)
½ tsp curd
1 tsp oil for cooking
½ tsp red chilli powder

Contd.

• Servings 5 persons • Preparation time 20 mins. • Cooking time 20 mins.
Per Serving Protein (gms) 15.8 • Fat (gms) .5 • Fibre (gms) 9 • Calories 90

- Sieve together oat bran, wheat bran, normal flour and salt. Add the husk back into the mixture.
- Mix *ajwain*, green chillies, ginger, ground *jeera, methi*, curd and oil. Gradually add water and make into a soft and smooth dough.
- Knead the dough for two or three minutes. Keep aside for 30 minutes.
- Divide the dough into five portions to make into round balls.
- Roll the round balls into five *chappatis.*
- Cook on a pre-heated greased *tava* (griddle) till golden brown on both sides.
- Soak a tablespoon of tamarind in water for half an hour,

Contd.

Water as required
½ cup finely chopped *methi* (fenugreek) leaves
Oil for greasing the *tava* (griddle)
Tamarind chutney

and extract the pulp. Cook this pulp with 4 tsp sugar, ½ tsp salt and ½ tsp red chilli powder to make tamarind chutney.

- Serve hot with beaten curd and the cooked tamarind chutney.

COCKTAIL-FRUIT STICKS

Ingredients
Strawberry sauce
½ cup strawberry, crushed
½ cup hung curd
1 tsp castor sugar
A dash of salt
A pinch of cardamom powder

Cocktail Sticks
10 to 12 wooden skewers
8 to 10 strawberries
4 pineapple slices
2 or 3 kiwi fruits
1 cup black or green grapes
Few chunks of mango or papaya
Few mint leaves

• Servings 8 persons • Preparation time 20 mins. • Cooking time 0 mins.
Per Serving Protein (gms) 3.5 • Fat (gms) .5 • Fibre (gms) 3 • Calories 20

- Mix together the crushed strawberry sauce, the hung curd, castor sugar, cardamom powder and a pinch of salt.
- Beat all the ingredients till smooth and creamy.
- Keep this in a bowl and garnish with mint leaves.
- Slice the strawberries lengthwise; cut out thick pineapple chunks and mango or papaya cubes. Peel kiwi fruit and cut into thick chunks.
- Now rinse the wooden skewers and thread strawberry, mango, kiwi, pineapple followed by grapes and mint leaves on to each stick.
- Similarly arrange all the sticks.
- Place strawberry sauce in a serving dish and arrange the fruit sticks all around it. Dip the fruit sticks in sauce when eating.

GLOSSARY

Aata	—	Whole wheat flour
Ajwain	—	Caraway seeds
Amchur	—	Dry mango powder
Anardana	—	Dry pomegranate seeds
Arhar dal/Toovar dal	—	A variety of lentil
Baigun	—	Brinjal (Aubergine and egg plant)
Besan	—	Gram flour
Channa dal	—	Black gram lentil
Chappati (Roti)	—	Indian wheat bread
Chirwa	—	Beaten rice
Dhokla	—	Fermented gram flour steamed cake
Garam masala	—	Ground spices for seasoning
Haldi	—	Turmeric
Hing	—	Asafoetida

Jeera	—	Cumin seeds
Kalonji	—	Onion seeds
Karahi	—	Pan for deep frying
Kasuri methi	—	A special type of dry fenugreek leaves
Katori	—	Small metal bowl
Khasta roti	—	A crisp Indian wheat bread
Khumb	—	Mushroom
Lobhia	—	Black eyed bean
Maida	—	Refined flour
Makai	—	Maize
Masala	—	Spice
Masoor dal	—	A variety of lentil (Pegion eyed lentil)
Mattar	—	Peas
Meetha soda	—	Soda bi-carb
Methi	—	Fenugreek
Missi roti	—	An Indian bread made from gram flour and wheat flour
Mooli	—	Radish

Moong dal	—	Green bean lentil
Paneer	—	Cottage cheese
Rajma	—	Kidney beans
Rava (Suji)	—	Semolina
Roomali roti	—	Paper thin wheat bread
Safed channa	—	Chickpeas
Saunf	—	Aniseeds
Suji	—	Semolina
Tandoor	—	Mud oven
Tandoori roti	—	Wheat bread baked in oven
Tava	—	Griddle
Tadka	—	Tempering
Thali	—	A round metal plate